D1472638

# Life's Riches

*Looking toward Fineview on Pittsburgh's North Side, with the West End Bridge of 1931 arching over the Ohio River.*

# Life's Riches

*Excerpts on the Pittsburgh Region
and Historic Preservation from the
Writings of Walter C. Kidney*

Pittsburgh History & Landmarks Foundation

Published by
Pittsburgh History & Landmarks Foundation
100 West Station Square Drive, Suite 450
Pittsburgh, PA 15219-1134
www.phlf.org

Text by Walter C. Kidney
Arranged and edited by Louise King Sturgess, with assistance from
Albert M. Tannler
Designed by Greg Pytlik of Pytlik Design Associates, Inc.

ISBN 0-9788284-0-2 (hard cover)
ISBN 0-9788284-1-0 (soft cover)
Library of Congress Control Number: 2006932941

Excerpts in *Life's Riches* were reprinted with permission. We thank:

• Allegheny County, for permission to reprint excerpts from
  *H. H. Richardson's Allegheny County Courthouse and Jail* (1981)

• Arcadia Publishing, for permission to reprint an excerpt from *Images of
  America: Oakland* (2005). The book is available from the publisher online
  at www.arcadiapublishing.com or by calling 888-313-2665.

• George Braziller, Inc., for permission to reprint an excerpt from
  *The Architecture of Choice: Eclecticism in America 1880–1930* (1974)

• The Society for Industrial Archeology, for permission to reprint excerpts
  from *Working Places: The Adaptive Use of Industrial Buildings* (1976)

Whenever possible, captions in *Life's Riches* were taken from works
by the author, published by the Pittsburgh History & Landmarks
Foundation, in order to maintain the author's voice.

*Life's Riches* was typeset in Fairfield and printed on Mohawk Options by
Friesens in Altona, Manitoba, Canada through Four Colour Imports, LTD.
Beth Buckholtz and Andrea Pytlik assisted with the design of the book.

Dedicated to
Richard Dilworth Edwards
(1919–2006), who, through his
steady influence as a trustee
of the Pittsburgh History &
Landmarks Foundation, inspired
us to discover, study, preserve,
adapt and *use* our architectural
heritage to enrich
life today.

# ILLUSTRATION SOURCES

© Albert Vecerka/Esto—Children's Museum of Pittsburgh: 60

Carnegie Library of Pittsburgh: 37, 91 *(photo by Clyde Hare)*

Carnegie Mellon University Archives: 45

John Conti: 19

Edwards family: vii

Clyde Hare: 18, 32, 40, 41, 43 (both), 59 (top right and bottom), 62, 67, 83

Jim Judkis: cover, iv, xiv, xviii, 2, 4, 5, 9, 13, 17, 21, 22, 24, 26, 27, 30, 35, 46, 54 (both), 57, 68, 71, 73, 75, 76, 86, 92

Pittsburgh City Photographer Collection, Archives Service Center, University of Pittsburgh: 29

Pittsburgh History & Landmarks Foundation: xii, 6, 10 (top), 11, 14, 15, 20, 25, 33, 38, 59 (top left), 61, 79

Pytlik Design Associates, Inc.: 12

Robert P. Ruschak: 64, 65

William Rydberg, PHOTON: xvi, 10 (bottom), 48, 49, 50, 51 (both), 52, 53, 55

## Acknowledgments

*Life's Riches* is a tribute to its author, the late Walter C. Kidney, who "wrote architectural history from the standpoint of historic preservation….from within an organization [the Pittsburgh History & Landmarks Foundation] committed to saving and maintaining historically significant buildings, neighborhoods, and landscapes," noted Albert M. Tannler, Historical Collections Director of the Foundation.

It is also evidence of the Pittsburgh History & Landmarks Foundation's commitment to architectural research, writing, and publishing. Since the founding of the organization in 1964, the Board of Trustees and President Arthur P. Ziegler, Jr. have encouraged a vigorous publications program. Seven of the ten books from which passages are taken to compose *Life's Riches* were, in fact, published by the Foundation.

Creating a publication is always a team effort, and I thank the following people for their advice and work. Reviewers of the manuscript included Laurie Cohen, Collection Services Librarian at the Hillman Library; Lu Donnelly, author and architectural historian; and David J. Vater, architect, and a trustee of the Pittsburgh History & Landmarks Foundation. Photographer Clyde Hare spent time finding just the right images for *Life's Riches* from his extensive historical collection. Jim Judkis took many new photographs that are especially sensitive to the author's words. For directions to the location from which the cover photo was taken, I thank Jack Miller, Director of Gift Planning at the Pittsburgh History & Landmarks Foundation. The view of Pittsburgh from St. John's Evangelical Lutheran Cemetery on the North Side has long been a favorite of Jack's.

*Life's Riches* is also available in compact disc form: the excerpts from the writings of Walter C. Kidney were recorded by SLB Radio

Productions on January 24, 2006 during a reading of the author's works. The favorable response of our members and friends to that event encouraged us to publish the excerpts as a book. As an elegant book took shape, it was a natural choice to dedicate it to trustee Richard D. Edwards, who died on June 26, 2006. A soft-spoken scholar of architectural history and persistent advocate for historic preservation, Dick took pleasure in elegant "built things." We thank Jamie Edwards and the Edwards family for their support and interest in our work.

The coming of the National Preservation Conference to Pittsburgh in 2006 provided us with the ideal time to release *Life's Riches*. We are especially grateful to Richard Moe, President of the National Trust for Historic Preservation, whose Foreword to this book simply and eloquently describes the lasting value of Walter's words.

Louise King Sturgess
*Executive Director*
*Pittsburgh History & Landmarks Foundation*

# Contributors

*Life's Riches* was funded by the Walter C. Kidney Library and Publications Fund of the Pittsburgh History & Landmarks Foundation, established through a bequest from Mr. Kidney and augmented by contributions from the following:

Allegheny Cemetery Historical Association
Anonymous
Arcadia Publishing Company
Jerome J. Balvo
Roger Beal
Mr. & Mrs. Walter J. Blenko, Jr.
David M. Brashear
Carl Wood Brown
Eliza Smith Brown
Albert T. and Anne S. Burgunder
John A. Burich
Barry L. Chad
E. Jane Colborn
Ann Connelly
Mary and John Davis
E. J. and Lu Donnelly
George and Eileen Dorman
Arthur J. Edmunds
Mr. & Mrs. William B. Eldredge
Marilyn J. Evert
Marc Finer, Communication Research, Inc.
Dr. & Mrs. William S. Garrett
Thomas H. Garver
Joan B. Gaul
Ed and Mary Ann Graf
Philip B. Hallen
Gretchen Haller
Marilyn P. Ham
Mr. & Mrs. John Campbell Harmon
Kathleen and Jared Heller
Gloria Henning
Suzanne W. Hershey
Eileen Hutchinson
William C. and Virginia A. Keck
Thomas and Pamela Keffer
Brent K. Lazar
Anne-Marie Lubenau

Mr. & Mrs. Bernard S. Mars
John A. Martine, AIA
Doug and Angela Marvin
Pamela and Jackson McCarter
Theodore C. Merrick
Donna and Jack Miller
Margaret J. Mima
Bill and Mary Anne Mistick
Louis Monterossi
Muriel R. Moreland
Mountvue Corporation
Dr. & Mrs. Holt Murray
Sue and S. A. Neff, Jr.
Eliza Scott Nevin
Mr. & Mrs. Thomas V. Pastorius
Lewis A. and Donna M. Patterson
Ray and Trevi Pendro
John and Marirose Radelet
Fred Rapone and Beth Pacoe
Audrey and Charles Reichblum
Carol Robinson and Jeffrey Markel
Stephen G. Robinson
Dr. & Mrs. Wilfred T. Rouleau
Barbara A. Ruane
Michael and Mary Leon Solomon
Frank Stroker
Louise King Sturgess
Elinor Szuch
Clarke M. Thomas
Lucille Cleeland Tooke
David J. Vater
Robert K. Wagner
Mrs. Frederick Walters
Mr. & Mrs. Robert B. Williams
Mary Wohleber
Carol Yaster and Bill Levant
Arthur P. Ziegler, Jr.

*Liverpool Street in Manchester, on Pittsburgh's North Side: identical double houses in the Second Empire style, all with delicately-detailed wooden entrance porches, form the city's most impressive house row.*

# CONTENTS

*Looking across the North Side of Pittsburgh toward the former H. J. Heinz plant, renovated as loft apartments in 2004.*

# FOREWORD

The late Walter C. Kidney was an architectural historian with a keen eye for the details and design nuances that make building-watching so enjoyable. He was also a writer of rare skills, an articulate raconteur who could blend fact with philosophy and turn prose into poetry. Those gifts are spotlighted in this jewel-like book, comprising excerpts from several of the author's works.

While he writes specifically about Pittsburgh, a city that he knew intimately and loved deeply, Kidney's words have a near-universal applicability. As he guides us through the streets of his hometown, he encourages us to explore the buildings, neighborhoods and landscapes that define and enrich our own communities. With scholarship and an occasional flash of humor, he helps us see the importance of the distinctive sense of place that makes every city—whether Pittsburgh or Palm Springs or Paris—unique and appealing.

Kidney is particularly insightful in his view of preservation's role in shaping community. "True preservation," he writes, "lets the city change, but change so that all the essential good of the past is saved...and new building is welcomed. The preservationist should thus concern himself with what is to be built as well as what has to be kept." It's an admonition that all of us should heed.

We thank the Pittsburgh History & Landmarks Foundation for publishing *Life's Riches* on the occasion of the National Preservation Conference 2006 and for giving conference attendees and others the opportunity to experience—and learn from—the genius of Walter C. Kidney.

Richard Moe
*President, National Trust for Historic Preservation*

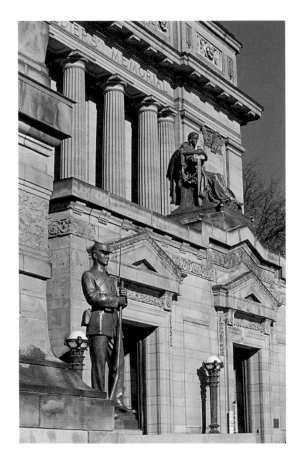

*Soldiers' and Sailors' National Military Museum
and Memorial (Palmer & Hornbostel, 1907–10),
4141 Fifth Avenue, Oakland.*

# LIFE'S RICHES

The excerpts that compose *Life's Riches* come from ten books by Walter C. Kidney, architectural historian of the Pittsburgh History & Landmarks Foundation from the 1980s until December 2005. They were compiled for a reading of the late author's works on January 24, 2006, at the Soldiers' and Sailors' National Military Museum and Memorial in Pittsburgh, Pennsylvania.

*Morning on South Linden Avenue in Pittsburgh's Point Breeze neighborhood.*

From *Pittsburgh's Landmark Architecture: The Historic Buildings of Pittsburgh and Allegheny County* (Pittsburgh History & Landmarks Foundation, 1997)

Bring to mind some good, long-held memories: Skies, tea-colored or purple in the west. The long, loud rasp of cicadas. The chirp of birds echoing between close-set walls. A house where time seemed to have eased to a halt around 1920. The bite of a winter evening when the streetcar was a long time coming. Lombardy poplars in a row on a hilltop. Quiet front-porch conversations, walks around the block, lamplight through the leaves. The smell of rain on cement, and the lindens turning up their gray-green leaves. Lighted windows seen through heavy rain. Ailanthus trees, and the pungent smell of their bruised leaves. Far away, the shouts of children beneath the white bulb of a streetlight in a dusty, weed-grown alley.

Oddly significant moments of one's life occur in such concrete circumstances, which themselves may sound meaningless. A building, a neighborhood paved in a certain way, lighted in a certain way, built up in a certain way, can be the occasion of such a personal moment in spite of itself, in a way beyond the possible calculations of an architect or planner....—*Page 195*

*Pittsburgh's South Side slopes and flats.*

Of our buildings generally, the greatest praise we can give is that they do not quarrel with our landscape when seen from afar. The building type most often seen in Allegheny County is the freestanding single-family house, and groupings of these, serrating the skyline of a hill, clinging to a distant slope, or riding the edges of a street that dips and rises with the land, dramatize the contours of the terrain and its great scale. They animate the space, reveal it as inhabited, and articulate the surfaces, otherwise winter-gray or summer-green with trees and shrubs, with their little white, cream, or red cubical forms. On the plateaus and river plains, where brick is more common than frame, they fall in orderly red rows, with the contrast here and there of a church, a school, a store, or an industrial building. So often of no account when seen up close, they become from afar the low-keyed brushstrokes on an Impressionistic canvas.

The real glory of the region, in fact, is its wonderful spaces, the vivid contours of the land and the sense of distance they create. From Mount Washington you can look out toward the South Side flats, 400 feet down and a mile-and-a-half away, still appearing like an independent town, but a town seen in some peculiar dream perspective hardly credible in a waking state; then look outwards toward the hill that rises behind, crowded with minute houses like white granules and see, behind the hip of land they occupy, a colossal silver cloud of steam rising from a coke plant hidden in the valley beyond. Or walk, again on

*Reaching into the sky on the 400-foot summit of Mount Washington.*

Mount Washington, down a colorless commercial street toward a void, with the tops of skyscrapers appearing strangely beyond its edge, and distant hilltops far beyond those; then look up and through a great red-and-white radio tower that rises, a little uncannily, from a lot by the street, and feel that you are inhabiting the sky rather than the ground. Or look out over the city at twilight, when the sun is just down, and see the shapes of buildings and hills begin to fade, tiny lights begin to glow, far away to the horizon, and get a poignant sense of human settlement, how it is spread wide but thin over the huge bulk of the earth.—*Pages 17–18*

*Pittsburgh at twilight, from the author's apartment on Mount Washington.*
*"The city is my night light," Walter said.*

*The 1200 block of Resaca Place, Mexican War Streets, North Side: saved through historic preservation efforts.*

Historic preservation has been a sort of Counter-Renaissance, not because the dusty city that Luke Swank knew is one that preservationists wish to keep frozen in time but because the progressives of the Renaissance too often ignored what was good about this city's past. They failed to see, certainly, that to break the continuity of a neighborhood's visible history, to sponge away whole streets of buildings, risks diminishing the inhabitants' sense of—their right, even, of sensing—who they are and what they are part of. If they are moved about arbitrarily, old associations are broken up, old friendships, old patterns of living. And how about the old architecture, considered purely as art? Has it perhaps touches of humanity in its detailing, perhaps concessions to human dignity in its deviations from the utilitarian, perhaps more positive visual effect in its color and texture, not to be found in what might replace it? Renaissance brought order, and a prosperity demonstrated in a way that attracted more prosperity, but it was not the most sensitive way of reshaping a city. It had to work fast, and there were penalties inherent in such speed.—*Page 166*

The same people who have supported historic preservation should find a means of intervening in design in the years to come: create a public demand, backed by informed ideas from architects and builders, for an architecture suited to the places where we live and the associations they have accumulated. This suggestion does not imply the imposition of a range of historic styles as happens in some preservation districts; unless modern demands are met with modern resources, with only limited artistic modification, the results will be unconvincing, shallow, and painfully artificial. Rather, it is made in the hope that the architecture we have in times to come will be a positive contribution, a thing from our own time that we can be proud of and that will add to, not be a subtraction from, what the past has left us.—*Pages 197 and 200*

*Artistry at Carnegie Mellon University: J. M. Hewlett's ceiling paintings at the College of Fine Arts, 5000 Forbes Avenue, Oakland.*

*Editor's Note: The following excerpts on individual historic structures are reprinted from the Guide section of* Pittsburgh's Landmark Architecture.

### Conestoga Building
*Wood Street and Fort Pitt Boulevard, Downtown*
*Longfellow, Alden & Harlow, architects, 1890*

Of stone, brown terra cotta, and golden-brown Roman brick, this is a sumptuously detailed, carefully studied building by the architectural firm that would soon be designing the first part of the Carnegie Institute. The loss of the cornice is a pity with everything else intact. The exterior is still traditional solid masonry construction, and is visibly divided into solid piers and screen walls of spandrels, mullions, and transoms set slightly back. The admirable care that was taken with details can easily be seen in the ground-floor openings. Not only do little corbels project to give token support to the lintels and help maintain the continuity of the masonry, but the edges of the corbels are carefully rounded in some parts and left sharp in others: an almost-invisible detail that adds a touch of life, a refinement of a refinement.—*Page 212*

## Arrott Building
*Fourth Avenue and Wood Street, Downtown*
*Frederick J. Osterling, architect, 1901–02;*
*Edward B. Lee, architect for remodeling of lower façades, 1928*

…Within the entrance arch is a lobby, tall, narrow, a little clumsy in overall design, but rich to the eye and full of character. Ornamental bronze and heavily-veined marble inlaid with Cosmati mosaic borders create an effect hard to describe. It is as if someone should descend that rather steep stair, hand trailing along the richly-worked balustrade, pause by the newel-post lamp on its four Ionic columns, and say something portentous, possibly reproachful.—*Page 218*

*A Victorian commercial building in Market Square, across from PPG Place (Philip Johnson with John Burgee, architects, 1979–84).*

## Market Square (originally the Diamond)
*Forbes Avenue and Market Street, Downtown*

...The architecture around the square and in the immediate area has been varied, in most cases of no distinction, and tending to be small-scaled. Yet it has color and variety, and compares well in this regard with the nearby central piazza of PPG Place, a despotic piece of total design. One wing of PPG Place actually fronts on Market Square, black and silver and of uniform upright elements, like a Prussian regiment formed up to impress the peasants.—*Page 224*

## Henry W. Oliver Building
*Smithfield Street and Oliver Avenue, Downtown*
*D. H. Burnham & Co. (Chicago), architects, 1908–10*

...The Oliver Building offers one extra pleasure, though, because of its unique situation: the pleasure of wondering over how good an architectural neighbor it is with the very different Trinity Cathedral. The secret is in the radicalism of the contrast. The cathedral is Gothic, blackened by Pittsburgh soot so that all its rich details are subordinated to a great shape that terminates in the grand gesture of the spire. The spire rises against the Oliver's sheer, glossy, gray-and-cream wall regularly perforated with windows not too much larger than those of a house, creating a broken but not restless pattern. The spire comes nowhere near the level of the office building's cornice; its scale is nonetheless greater than that of the office building façade. It is a big thing against a background of small things whose number no one will bother to count. Neither building disparages the other; they are in contiguous, different, but compatible worlds.—*Page 235*

*Trinity Cathedral, 328 Sixth Avenue, downtown (Gordon W. Lloyd, Detroit, 1870–71) and the Henry W. Oliver Building.*

*The interior of the Mellon Bank building was destroyed in 1999 for the short-lived Lord & Taylor department store: it closed in 2004.*

## Mellon Bank

*Fifth Avenue and Smithfield Street, Downtown*
*Trowbridge & Livingston (New York), architects;*
*E. P. Mellon (New York), associate architect, 1923–24*

In a way this is the architectural equivalent of the rich lady's simple but expensive dress. In the gray granite exterior there is no ostentation, just dignity and self-respect. But: in an area of tall buildings, this is only four stories high; this place of money casually throws away the rentals from fifteen to twenty possible stories of upper office space. Inside there is nothing flamboyant about the banking room, sixty-two feet high, lined with beige marble and with marble Ionic columns with gilded capitals.—*Page 236*

Chalfant house (now Chalfant Hall, Community College
of Allegheny County, Allegheny Campus)
*915 Ridge Avenue, Allegheny West*
*C. 1900*

Many well-to-do or rich Pittsburghers around 1900 built new
houses such as this. The human parallel might be a serious,
preoccupied man who dresses correctly for a social occasion
without feeling social. The golden-brown Roman brick is a fine
material, the porch in an unfluted Grecian Ionic order is very
handsome, and the Federal-style ironwork above it is quite
delicate. These and other individual features could have been
elements of a forthcoming and even witty design. And yet this
house is grave in effect as so many large Pittsburgh houses are;
the local genius could make Georgian feel like Romanesque. But this is not to disparage the Chalfant house, which
has character and invites the passer-by to speculate on the
lives that were spent within its slightly brooding depths.
—*Page 268*

**Liberty Tunnels ventilating plant**
*201 Secane Avenue, Mount Washington*
*Stanley L. Roush, architect, 1928*

...In 1928 a mechanical plant with four tall stacks was built over the center of the [Liberty] Tubes. The material is a bright-red brick with limestone detailing, and the style is a bland quasi-Gothic manner. The four great stacks could not have been more fortunately placed from a scenic point of view; their powerful forms thrust upward from the shelf-like spur of the hillside on which the plant stands, in dramatic contrast with the broad valley spaces around them, framing views of distant hillsides, contrasting their simple surfaces with the tiny-looking houses and trees beyond and their vivid redness with the more neutral colors of the landscape.—*Pages 303–304*

### South Side Public Baths (Oliver Bath House)
*South Tenth and Bingham Streets, South Side flats*
*MacClure & Spahr, architects, 1915*

As was the case with the contemporary Sarah Heinz House, a Tudoresque manner was used to clothe a philanthropic gift to the workers. It was a little pompous, a little genteel perhaps, but it was also home-like. Its mellow, textured red brick with raked joints was in marked contrast with the prevalent hard industrial surfaces, and plunging dolphins on the buttress tops hinted at the bodies of water within.—*Page 315*

**Longue Vue Club**
*Oakwood Road, Penn Hills Township*
*Janssen & Cocken, architects, 1924–25; additions*

There is a nice ambiguity about the style of the original club building. The big chimneys, flush with the gable walls, could be Georgian, yet the overall feeling is that of French rural architecture, a feeling heightened by the use of casement windows. This is the suave rusticity often found in Philadelphia-area architecture of the 1920s, but much less often in Southwestern Pennsylvania: long, slender pieces of rubble in thick mortar, the masonry equivalent of a good hand-woven tweed, and above, thick, rough-edged roofing slates. A building as unornamented as any Modern work, it still conveys a lush impression through its picturesque exaggerations of form and texture.—*Page 597*

*The main entrance road passes through a tunnel that bridges two portions of the clubhouse.*

Less frequent than the bridges, less conspicuous in the landscape but striking nonetheless, are the great Victorian retaining walls that appear here and there where the right-of-way for a street or railroad has been cut from a hillside. Until the 1900s, like bridge piers and abutments of the time, these were typically made of massive, rugged-textured, roughly-squared stones, which if the stonecutters were on piecework might have their personal symbols scratched on the surfaces. Such walls, which may be fifty feet high and hundreds of feet in length, made of the gray sandstone turned a soft black under the Pittsburgh soot, are impressive in their rugged texture, their perceptible mass. The distinctive Romanesque of Henry Hobson Richardson, once it appeared in downtown Pittsburgh in the Allegheny County Courthouse and Jail (1884–88), was imitated in churches and commercial buildings for a decade, perhaps because it was simply a refinement of the raw engineering masonry that the city had known for years.—*Pages 8–9*

*A Pennsylvania Railroad retaining wall below West Carson Street on Pittsburgh's South Side, in a view of 1930.*

FROM *H. H. Richardson's Allegheny County Courthouse and Jail* (ALLEGHENY COUNTY BUREAU OF CULTURAL PROGRAMS, 1981)

Richardson, who loved to design a tower, gave the Courthouse one that was simple and strong in its general outline, delicate in its detail, a solid mass seen from some angles and strangely transparent seen from others. At its foot he put three cavernous entrances with arches of rugged stone, then set off this massive simplicity with finely-carved sculpture. In the courtyard he did another essay in arches, big and little, marching with dignity along the walls or climbing as if endlessly up the stair towers. Throughout the Courthouse exterior he played off vigorously-textured surfaces against hard, smooth ones, with here and there a sculptured accent....—*Page* 20 (*unnumbered*)

*H. H. Richardson's Allegheny County Courthouse (1884–88), 436 Grant Street. The Courthouse tower has not dominated Pittsburgh for a hundred years, but its simple, slender, strong form rises among towers much taller, and among them is an aristocrat.*

*Masonry composition in space: Richardson's grand stair in the Allegheny County Courthouse.*

*Two powerful statements of differing modes of construction: the Ross Street face of the Courthouse expresses solid masonry as eloquently as the U.S. Steel Building, in the background, expresses the steel frame.*

In 1890 the tower of the Courthouse, a pale gray shaft rising among church spires and above commercial buildings, dominated the city. Not for long; from 1901 on the Frick Building confronted the Courthouse, its slablike form and its smooth, simply detailed granite walls almost like a cool aristocratic snub to the romantic towers, roofs and dormers, the carved ornament, the vigorous textures of the older building....When the Courthouse tower was proposed, Richardson rationalized it as the intake for what was to be almost a central air-conditioning system, and as a place for the archives. The truth, most likely, is that everyone understood it as the grand rhetorical gesture expected of the courthouse of a prosperous county. The sheer quantity of business construction around it has ended its domination of the city, yet its quality is apparent and undiminished. It is one of the world's great towers. It is useless, and modernist critics, with their utilitarian bias, either deplore or ignore it. But its claim to existence is that of any work of art.

—*Page 22 (unnumbered)*

*From within the Courthouse courtyard, Richardson's Romanesque tower seems to surpass D. H. Burnham's Frick Building of 1901.*

FROM THE LAST PAGE OF *Images of America: Oakland*
(ARCADIA PUBLISHING, 2005)

We end with a final contrast, one of architecture from the
beginning of Pittsburgh's City Beautiful campaign with that of
its climax—and, for that matter, of its effective end. The Hotel
Schenley, brown brick and terra cotta, is finished off with the
emphatic horizontal of a jutting, fretted cornice [now gone]—
still a Victorian building, rather phlegmatic in expression if
elaborate in detail. It was a worldly building of its time.
Behind it is the Cathedral of Learning, a strange, fanciful
Gothic essay of complex, ascending masses faced in white
limestone, a work of fictitious arches and abutments, a sort of
habitable expressionist sculpture of courage and spirituality,
victory and adventure: a dream.—*Page 128*

*The Hotel Schenley (Rutan & Russell, 1898) and Cathedral of Learning
(Charles Z. Klauder, 1926–37) are part of the University of Pittsburgh's
Oakland campus. The Hotel Schenley is now the William Pitt Student
Union.*

From *Pittsburgh's Bridges: Architecture and Engineering*
(Pittsburgh History & Landmarks Foundation, 1999)

A bridge is a means of connecting separate places on the same
level that can be crossed absent-mindedly, unnoticing. It also
can be a handsome work of structural art or a piece of visual
rhetoric, granted. But there are other ways of perceiving it.
Sonically, a bridge can be a living thing. You are standing on a
river shore, and far above you is a bridge, with traffic briskly
passing over an expansion joint: pa-*pum*, pa-*pum*…pa-*pum*…
pa-*pum* pa-*pum* pa-*pum*, and so on. You are in an excursion
boat, approaching then passing under a bridge, and the echoes
of the parted waters and engine beat go into a crescendo, then
a diminuendo, from the bridge's floor and piers. A bridge, too,
is a means of screening a distant landscape, cutting off a long
perspective, controlling through its structural work how much
you see and dividing it into fragments of color and geometry.
Crossing a valley, it imposes form and scale, a shape to the void

*Silhouettes and the city, seen from the Roberto Clemente Bridge spanning
the Allegheny River (Allegheny County Department of Public Works,
engineers; Stanley L. Roush, architect; 1926–28).*

*The arch in concrete: the George Westinghouse Memorial Bridge over Turtle Creek Valley (Allegheny County Department of Public Works, engineers; George S. Richardson, principal designer; 1930–32).*

that states where the walled space ends and the sky begins. Finally, a great bridge, high above a valley, can create a wonderful feeling of There versus Here. You are on a valley floor, looking up at the stately row of illuminated bridge lamps, showing the way between places not seen. Or you are standing on a bridge on a summer evening, looking at a little neighborhood 100 feet below, hearing the shouts of children whose running forms appear under a corner street lamp, a world away down there.—*Page 10*

*Five distinct structural types span the Monongahela River in about one-and-a-half river miles, beginning with the lenticular truss Smithfield Street Bridge (Gustav Lindenthal, engineer; 1881–83), connecting downtown Pittsburgh with Station Square.*

FROM *The Three Rivers* (PITTSBURGH HISTORY & LANDMARKS FOUNDATION, 1982)

Pittsburgh's beauty is in its spaces: in the many chances there are, in and around the city, to look down, or up, or away, and see clustered houses, shrubs, and trees, hills like tossing waves, fretted skylines of roofs and chimneys, ridges beyond ridges under a variegated light as the clouds pass over. No great matter if you are—and you probably are—standing at the edge of a dreary street, looking, if you only knew, toward a multitude of other dreary streets: the distances are great enough, and the contours of the land are overmastering enough, that you are encouraged to imagine that over *there* it is all beautiful.

And the rivers, which long ago carved the hills, give vitality to the whole scene as the most overmastering element of all. They appear in different colors, and odd textures cover parts of their surfaces, apparently without cause. Sometimes they are slick as wax, sometimes minutely ruffled like a silver-gray felt, sometimes blown into little waves, sometimes marbled with ice. The surface quality of the land changes slowly with the seasons for the most part, but the surface of a river, seen from a hillside, is different from one day to the next.—*Page 72*

*Water textures: morning on the Monongahela River.*

FROM *The Architecture of Choice: Eclecticism in America 1880–1930* (GEORGE BRAZILLER, INC., 1974)

...The Eclectic saw himself as a participant in, or an heir to, a reform movement that had restored taste and literacy to architecture. Unlike the mid-Victorian, the Eclectic studied all aspects of the style in which he proposed to design not just the standard ornamental motifs, but the scale, proportions, massing, colors, and textures. These things contributed, in varying degrees, to the true look of the style. Once his contribution was assessed, the Eclectic felt free to introduce variations of his own: to abbreviate or suppress typical ornamental details, even to create original ones; to substitute a new material for an "authentic" one. By a skillful adjustment of the elements and by careful detailing he could create something marginally original, yet free of any feeling of incongruity, relying on his sense of how the style of choice worked visually....—*Page* 3

*The casual attitude of an Eclectic toward structural truth: masonry expression, steel construction. The College of Fine Arts at Carnegie Tech (Carnegie Mellon University), designed by Henry Hornbostel, 1912–13; 1915–16.*

*At the end of his cross-corridor at the College of Fine Arts, Eclectic architect Henry Hornbostel had a raised area screened by Tuscan columns, purely it appears to soften the terminations of this long passage.*

A new look at Eclecticism, one with an openness to the pleasure that it might offer us today, will probably depend as much on our understanding the Eclectic architect and his client as human beings as it does on our readiness to consider the artistic merits of a revived architecture or our willing suspension of disbelief regarding certain arches and beams. Eclecticism is one of those phases in architectural history when the human factor was involved most conspicuously, one whose works are beyond a certain point incomprehensible without understanding and lending sympathy to an earlier generation, its society, and its attitudes. If we can establish that the Eclectic architect and his client were not two-dimensional monsters, and that Eclectic architecture was at its best a carefully considered, fully appreciated response to the cultural values architect and client shared, then we can be less inhibited about investigating what the forms, colors, and textures of Eclectic architecture have to offer us, seeing all things even with the eyes of our own time.—*Page 68*

FROM *Henry Hornbostel: An Architect's Master Touch*
(PITTSBURGH HISTORY & LANDMARKS FOUNDATION, 2002)

Hornbostel was an Eclectic, in the sense that the term was used early in the twentieth century. That is, he was ready to take compositional ideas from the past if it suited his purpose. He might also devise a building that was quite without precedent; it was a matter of what expressed the role and suited the location of the work. The president of Carnegie Tech had his office in a building of industrial brick composed to an Italian Renaissance formula, but lived in a house that imitated dry stone rubble construction, set against a hillside: both buildings

*Hornbostel's Central, or Administration Building, of 1914, now Baker Hall at Carnegie Mellon University, Oakland.*

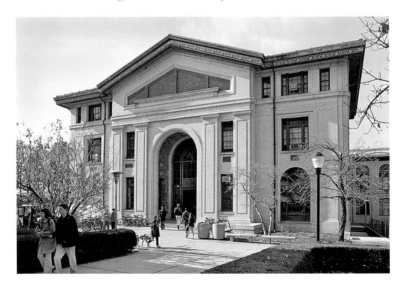

*"Ledge House" (4040 Bigelow Boulevard, Schenley Farms) was designed c. 1909 by Henry Hornbostel for Carnegie Tech president Arthur A. Hamerschlag.*

by Hornbostel. He designed two synagogues for Pittsburgh, and a church: the first two were massive in volume, hinting at the Near East, the last a wiry Gothic using several European national manners. He designed such places when Modernism, with its moralistic fervor, was calling for Truth: truth to our period of history, truth to the functional requirements of a building, truth to its materials and structural system. Hornbostel was not one of the duller Eclectics who passively relied on a style and did little more than copy. He used his schooling and acquaintance with historic architecture in a creative, innovative, and bold manner....—*Page 5*

*Smithfield United Church (1925–26), 620 Smithfield Street, downtown.*

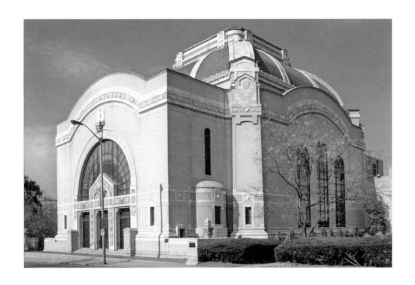

*Two synagogues by Hornbostel: the cream-colored brick-and-terra cotta*
*Rodef Shalom Congregation (1906–07), 4905 Fifth Avenue in Shadyside,*
*and the dark stone-and-brick Congregation B'nai Israel (1923–27),*
*327 North Negley Avenue in East Liberty, now owned by the Urban*
*League of Pittsburgh Charter School.*

City-County Building
*414 Grant Street, Downtown*
*Edward B. Lee and Palmer, Hornbostel & Jones, associated architects,*
*1915–17*

*The Grant Street front.*

...This great passage is light and airy, looking out to light court walls of off-white brick and white terra-cotta ornament. It has an intriguing ambiguity: you are inside the passage, but inside the light court too, and thus in a sense outside. Tunnel-like passages lead off openings in the marble wainscot to ground-floor offices. The treatment is grandly civic in its public spaces, yet at times almost modern in a no-nonsense way, suitable for a government building that has left behind Victorian towers to look like an efficient office block. Yet there is subtle detailing, such as the cyma reversa, rounded off at the top, that crowns the marblework. And splashes of outright ornament. Here the gilt-bronze corridor columns, Classical in feeling but almost without precedent and with richly-figured

*The barrel-vaulted ground-floor corridor of the City-County Building, just before security enclosures were installed. The windows at the corridor ends have double thicknesses of glass, with the floor plates between them, so that people passing from side to side seem to be striding on air.*

*The sculptured base of the gilt-bronze columns and an elevator door detail.*

lower parts, are conspicuous, as are the elevator doors in high relief that show three Allegheny County Courthouses and three Pittsburgh City Halls. But there are also delicate hanging lanterns and sockets for low-power exposed lightbulbs in foliated bronze, and sculptural drinking fountains. Upstairs, the City Council Chamber and other prestigious places are treated richly with inlaid woodwork, stencil work, and richly-molded plaster.

In all, you have a building of contrasts that work together beautifully: the multi-windowed steel cage with its clear surfaces, the great spaces, bursts of lavish ornamentation, and little subtleties of treatment that liven it more and more as you get to know it.—*Pages 144–145*

*The portico of the City-County Building is vaulted in Guastavino tile, in two shades, in a fish-scale pattern.*

From *Working Places: The Adaptive Use of Industrial Buildings* (The Society for Industrial Archeology and Ober Park Associates, Inc., 1976)

America, at least in its attitude toward material wealth, may be undergoing a major psychological change....

From thinking it beneath us, as Americans, to re-use a building (or a beer can) once its intended role is played out, we may bend our ingenuity, rather, to see how far some man-made object or material can serve a whole succession of purposes, none of which may have any ostensible relation to the others. "Adhocism" has recently become a fashionable word, but it refers to an ancient practice, that of seeing an object not as a means to a narrow and theoretical end but as a thing with certain properties adapting it to a variety of ends. Thus, a chair is an object to sit upon *and* a platform, a ladder, a footrest, a clothes rack, and so forth.

Our use of a chair in this way is instinctive. Our use of an industrial building as a school, an apartment house, a company headquarters, or what have you, is not. A blend of imagination and calculation is needed to germinate the idea and make it work. But this blend is appearing more and more, among pragmatic developers as well as preservationists.—*Pages 3 and 4*

*The Grand Concourse Restaurant at Station Square occupies the main floor of the former Pittsburgh & Lake Erie Railroad Terminal Building (William George Burns, architect, 1901).*

FROM *A Past Still Alive: The Pittsburgh History &*
*Landmarks Foundation Celebrates Twenty-five Years*
(PITTSBURGH HISTORY & LANDMARKS FOUNDATION, 1989)

...The past and the future are like a cable formed from strands
of varying length and prominence that overlap so that, barring
some violent severing, they form a continuity regardless of
wherever individual strands may end or begin. True preservation will understand this. To most of us, Pittsburgh is home.
Things change, in our own little world as individuals, family
members, or residents of a neighborhood, and in the larger
world of the whole city. Much of the change is at least
acceptable, some of it is positively desirable, and if we are
lucky the changes are not so radical that we become disorient-
ed and wonder where our home has gone. Preservation,
properly understood, understands that there *will* be a future
and seeks to integrate with this future those things from the
past that have been especially good and familiar and beautiful:
specific buildings and other places in some instances; in
other instances ways of building, of using the land, general
characteristics of the physical environment that are the
preservationist's special domain.—*Pages 79–80*

*Architectural patterns, historical overlaps: downtown Pittsburgh scenes.*

...Yet there is a danger of artificiality and contrivance about conventional historic preservation, of forced make-believe, just as there was danger from starry-eyed money-chasing or standardized do-gooding in the conventional urban renewal that historic preservation arose, as a major force, to combat. The preservationist must not drag his protected structures into the future, there to drift as indigestible lumps in a world to which they have no relevance, for some vaguely-conceived "ever after."

Rather, he must know that what he will fight to protect has a place and a meaning in the future....—*Page 80*

*The Children's Museum of Pittsburgh on the North Side connects 19th- and 20th-century landmarks with a 21st-century structure.*

Historic preservation, then, appears these days to go beyond the saving of specific buildings and other places for specific, positive reasons. It is a reactionary movement, literally, a defense against drab, dumb construction of the sort all too likely to happen or against, indeed, the coming-to-be of yet another parking lot where at least passable architecture has stood. But we should be doing what we can to see that there is no cultural need to preserve less than the most distinguished places from the past. Our ideal should be a state of things in which we can anticipate new works of building, planning, and development with confidence that they will be at least as beautiful and heart-warming as what they replace.—*Page 84*

*What one can normally expect from an ordinary builder is quite different now from what it was a century or two ago. The Oliver Miller Homestead (1808 and 1830) in South Park shows the Georgian architecture of this region in its simplest form: undecorated but orderly and well proportioned.*

*The Landmarks Building (formerly the Pittsburgh & Lake Erie Railroad Terminal Building) at Station Square is illuminated at night, with the Golden Triangle beyond.*

...True preservation lets the city change, but change so that all the essential good of the past is saved, even augmented, and new building is welcomed on the condition that this happens.

The preservationist should thus concern himself with what is to be built as well as what has to be kept. His knowledge and his interests will be limited, but within his limits he can be a scholar, an ideologue, and a propagandist in a general movement to maintain and improve a community that continues to be home to its inhabitants.—*Page 85*

Of architecture we do indeed have handsome examples, just as we have our monuments and our structures and places that there is reason to preserve. But apart from a few isolated places, the continuing visual character of Pittsburgh will depend on a sense of Man in the terrain, the way he builds, the means he uses to impose his will on the stubborn contours of the land. The architecture of the future, which can perpetuate or mar this visual character, will depend on the demands of the evolving social and economic character of the community; and the ways in which we build and in which we occupy the land may alter to meet the new demands. We must be ready, maintaining continuity in the midst of change.—*Pages 89–90*

Man and Nature have had an uneasy coexistence around Pittsburgh. When heavy industry flourished, its structure rivaled the hills themselves for prominence on the scene. Nature in the form of vegetation withdrew entirely in some places, as it did at Hazelwood when the beehive coke ovens poisoned the air. But Nature was always waiting to come back, always sneaking in an ailanthus or a clump of weeds in some untraveled part of the industrial property, and now that the industrial plants are so largely shut down it is reveling among the ponderous machines and even within the vast sheds.
—*Page 93*

*The thriving Edgar Thomson Works in North Braddock at night, November 1988, and the abandoned Duquesne Works and Dorothy furnaces in Duquesne, October 1989.*

...Despite its present picturesque details, our city needs to be improved as a functioning mechanism, and the Veterans' Bridge and I-279 show how unfeelingly we now attack the larger aspects of the problem. Our modernization attempts in the past have offended the eyes with painted brickwork, applied shakes, fake shutters, and the conspicuous absence of many front porches. We should be able to do better, and unless we wish gradually to give up the use of our eyes except as informational and navigational devices we will have to do better. An understanding of what is good in that which we have now is the way to begin.—*Page 114*

*The Veterans' Bridge of 1987 dwarfs the historic bridges over the Allegheny River and merges with I-279 on Pittsburgh's North Side.*

*Brereton Street in Polish Hill.*

From *Beyond the Surface: Architecture and Being Alive*
(PITTSBURGH HISTORY & LANDMARKS FOUNDATION, 2006)

## DAYBREAK

Suppose, that long ago, you awoke too early. You had floated, or had been expelled, from one of the innumerable realms of the night into a version of your daily world. It was still dark, but the birds had begun their rhythmic chirping. Far off, road traffic whirred quietly, and perhaps a locomotive or a towboat sounded its horn—or was it a steam whistle, so long ago? The architectures of the street were mere patterns, black and whatever color of light the lamps afforded. The world, such as it was, was yours. Then there were voices on the walk, car doors slamming, a sound of driving away. First light began to come, and the distant traffic started to give out a richer and louder sound, a tuning-up of the new day. Façades began to acquire definition; moldings and brackets, brickwork and wooden siding took on depth and color. Chipped stone, dented sheet metal, flaked paint exaggerated their blemishes in the warm morning light, then dissembled them as the sun went higher. Gradually the pomps of the street architecture took on their intended definition of full daylight. At last, it was clearly time to be up and doing; you were no longer the solitary lord of this new morning, but one being among many.—*Page 15*

## Starting to Look Around

When you are a child, your eyes are close to the ground. Furthermore, you have yet to acquire an adult's sense of Important and unimportant. Chalk marks on a pavement or the signs painted on the roadway by utility workers: there is something about little things like those that can give keen enjoyment. Or the blackish-green stains made on a stone by rubbing fresh ailanthus leaves on it. (In my memory, the pungent smell of bruised ailanthus leaves is the very smell of summer and a happy past.) Or such a modest thing as a builder's attempt to add a little grace to a commonplace job—intended for the adult eye but never quite real to such eyes, conditioned as they are to the adult world of cares, fashions, and dismissals. The intensity of pleasure in such simple things, in the reality that they can have, is incredible to remember when you grow older. Even experiences that at the time seemed boring or miserable may seem in retrospect to have had something like beauty. There may have been attendant things about the experience, maybe irrelevant by any rational standard, that stayed with you: the moldings and color of a door

*A stonecutter's mark on the Panther Hollow Bridge, constructed in 1897 over Junction Hollow in Oakland.*

and its frame, the colors and pattern of a lampshade. Something not visual, perhaps, not pleasant even, but flavorful, like a peculiar word spoken in a context of anger.

And so much to learn. I find myself using the image of the chameleon: and not for its ability to change appearance. A chameleon has a long, curling tongue that opens full-length until an insect morsel drifts by, then winds it in with a snap. Facts that chance to drift by should be snapped up in a similar way if they promise flavor, even if no particular nourishment. Consider, for instance, that strange design-related field called heraldry, where the jazzy achievements of arms and the bizarre Anglo-Norman jargon describing them are both beguiling. A disk, for instance, can be a bezant, plate, torteau, hurt, golp, guze, gunstone, ogress, pellet, fountain, or gurge, depending on color or pattern. And the escutcheon of Pittsburgh is blazoned: Sable, a fess chequy argent and azure between three bezants charged with an eagle displayed or. Such information is almost certainly not Important to you, but such things season the meal of life.—*Pages 18–21*

*The City escutcheon, on the portal of the Smithfield Street Bridge, down-town. The portals of 1915, designed by City Architect Stanley Roush, replaced the original ones of 1883.*

## BUILT THINGS

Perhaps it was a reassuring sense of order in the world around that led me to a thrill with built things. Not just buildings but works of civil engineering, ships, locomotives, stationary engines. Some people would add smaller and subtler things too: watches, furniture, any sort of put-together human contrivance. At the start, in my case, there was that big model of the full-rigged ship *Ocean Monarch* at the Carnegie Institute. There was the excursion steamer *Senator*, and those long summer cruises, looking at the Ohio River and the towns drifting past, listening to "Sunrise Serenade" or whatever the band was playing and now and then going to watch the engines, with their big pitmans, as they turned the sidewheels. And later in my life the Hudson River sidewheeler *Alexander Hamilton*, with its inclined triple-expansion engine that again I could watch up close. There was that 1930s film *Swiss Family Robinson*, forgettable except for the graceful ship that got wrecked. And the Great White Fleet that appeared in Webster's Third International with such other accomplishments of 1910 America as a streetcar (still made of wood) and a skyscraper (300 feet high, about) that looked more or less like the Oliver Building on Smithfield Street in Pittsburgh. There were even those juvenile books on Iron Men and Wooden Ships, far from the sea though I was and short on illustrations though they were. Built things. The glamorous hardware of civilization.—*Pages 25–26*

*Built things:* the American Queen *docked at the Monongahela wharf, with Fort Pitt Boulevard and downtown buildings beyond.*

*Entrance detail, Carnegie Library of Pittsburgh (Longfellow, Alden & Harlow; 1892–95), 4400 Forbes Avenue, Oakland.*

## Such a Thing as Architecture

People create autolegends (analogous with autobiographies), deciding long afterward that their lives have had this or that Great Moment. One of mine is that, some time before age ten, I was on a neighbor's porch and noticed the Roman Ionic capitals on the posts. I suspected then that there was such a thing as architecture, and when I was taken to the Carnegie Library of Pittsburgh for the first time, I *knew* that there was such a thing as architecture. The round arches, the pilasters and keystones, the bronze masks and fish-scale patterns over the doors, the orderly rhythm of piers and vaults inside, all spoke of a rational, lavish, benign world, calm though with room for fantasy in its manner of existence.—*Page 26*

## Thoughts of an Afternoon

I ended up not practicing architecture, not researching its history in a methodical way: just an aesthete, moved by some buildings and some places, and thinking about built things and their significance in the whole experience of being alive....
—*Page 43*

## Characterizing Architecture

When we apply the word "architecture" to something built, we intend to praise it. There is a feeling about it of being as it is (and, quite possibly, where it is) for good reason. It has a special presence because of the look of its surfaces, its massing, its skyline, the experience of its spaces as you pass through them—their proportions, their light, their openness, their acoustics, the changes of level or direction. It communicates moods and shares associations, using symbols such as Gothic arches, or massive chimneys thrusting through great sheltering roofs. Sometimes its size, its massing, its ornamentation express the public significance of its function. Sometimes it seems to be attempting magic, imparting a sense of transcendent order and significance in an otherwise casual, meaningless place. At the least, it makes some sort of sense. The dimensions and arrangement of its spaces, its ability to shelter, its overall convenience and durability are adequate, let us hope, but never taken for granted; works of artistry in building sometimes claim admiration and love in spite of their performances as shelter.—*Page 56*

*Gothic in the Commons Room of the Cathedral of Learning, University of Pittsburgh (Charles Z. Klauder, 1926–37), Oakland.*

## Body and Soul

Let me indulge myself in a little irrationality on the ways that things, without souls, can nevertheless seem alive....

Imagine a city you could swear was alive, a place where the living population, the citizens that once were there, and the constructions and spaces of the town were in an interaction that made the whole place almost a living being. The word "great" would be wrong for such a city—that has an air of braggadocio about it, and size, wealth, or power would not be enough to give it its particular magic. Perhaps "classic" would be better, since the city would be uniquely and splendidly itself. Its countless inanimate features and its populations past and existing would be a perceived essence, sometimes thrilling, sometimes homelike and sustaining, never to be reduced to formula and imitated.

Perhaps you can use an analogy drawn from the Pittsburgh of a century ago. Imagine a beehive coke oven, where a charge of coal, being refined into coke for blast furnace fuel, smoldered in a meager allowance of air until it was ready to be raked out. A new charge of coal, dumped into the oven, would take fire from the accumulated heat and would start smoldering in its turn. So with this city: new material, catching fire from the past and imparting its heat to material even newer.

To have just moved to a new city is almost like having to learn a new branch of technology. The bads and the goods and the caveats; the wheres and whos and hows; the streets, the squares, the names of places: a galaxy of strange things that the newcomer has to absorb, and who has the pleasure as well as the burden of learning them. His ears may pick up a richer sound than can those who have heard the local music all their lives.

If your beloved home should collapse, you might be crushed. The place is made of heavy, lifeless material, after all, merely shaped, assembled, and finished in certain ways. But if the ways are the right ones and if your spirit can give this lifeless assemblage the chance, this *will* be a home, your little world within the world, and "lifeless" then seems not to be an applicable word.—*Pages 65–67*

## Time Passes

I ended up in historic preservation, which seeks to keep specific places, and some types of places, that have meant something to a community, that have been elements of its beauty or character, or reminders of its history: places whose loss would lessen the intimacy between the physical community and those who know and love its continuing if changing essence, even if there were no loss of national or world culture.

But in any one case there is always the question, voiced or not, of *how long* you will preserve the place, and at what sacrifice....

Perhaps a reasonable conclusion is: preserve good old architecture, preserve memories, let things flow slowly, apply the brakes to change selectively. Continue creating, of course, and keep on learning, finding, and enjoying life's riches as you can. And try to see in the whole thing a meaning.—*Pages 81–82*

*St. Michael's Cemetery on the South Side and innumerable little houses,
with the towers of Pittsburgh's Golden Triangle not far beyond.*

# THE AUTHOR

*Walter C. Kidney (1932–2005), photographed in 1999 amidst page proofs of his book,* Pittsburgh's Bridges: Architecture and Engineering.

# The Author

Walter Curtis Kidney, Jr. was born January 24, 1932, in Johnstown, Pennsylvania, to Mona Jeannerat and Walter C. Kidney. The family moved to Philadelphia in 1942 when Walter's father accepted a position as a teacher of Greek and Latin. Summers, however, were spent in Pittsburgh's Oakland neighborhood where Walter's grandparents lived.

Between 1942 and 1961, Walter lived in Philadelphia and in its Main Line suburbs, Haverford, Bryn Mawr, and Radnor. He attended Haverford College and was graduated with a Bachelor's degree in Philosophy in 1954. Subsequently, he worked for a time as a library assistant at The Athenaeum of Philadelphia, known for its architectural collections.

In 1961 he joined the staff of Random House, Inc. in New York City where he was employed for the next six years as a dictionary editor. In 1967–68 he worked as a researcher and writer for *Progressive Architecture* magazine. He moved to Cleveland in 1968 to accept an editorial position at The Press of Case Western Reserve University, which he held until 1973. (In 1971, Walter's father retired and his parents moved to Pittsburgh.) Walter lived in Pittsburgh from 1973 to 1976, working as a free-lance writer/editor, and then lived in Essex, Connecticut from 1976 to 1978, working as an editor for Laurence Urdang, Inc. He returned to Pittsburgh in 1978.

From the early 1980s until his death on December 1, 2005, Walter served as an architectural historian and author for the Pittsburgh History & Landmarks Foundation, first on a free-lance basis and beginning in 1988 as a full-time employee. As the author and editor of more than twenty significant publications on local history and architecture, Walter helped shape the philosophy of the Pittsburgh History & Landmarks Foundation. He saw historic preservation as a way to maintain "continuity in the midst of change" so a community could continue to be home to its inhabitants. Through his insightful, graceful prose, Walter helped people see inanimate objects in "animate" ways.

Walter's first book, *Historic Buildings of Ohio*, was published in 1972. Two years later *The Architecture of Choice: Eclecticism in America 1880–1930* was published and is today recognized as a pioneering assessment and defense of an architectural language then widely despised. Seventeen books on architectural history and historic places and structures followed. His later major works, all published by the Pittsburgh History & Landmarks Foundation, included *A Past Still Alive* (1989); *Allegheny Cemetery: A Romantic Landscape in Pittsburgh* (1991); *Pittsburgh's Landmark Architecture: The Historic Buildings of Pittsburgh and Allegheny County* (1997), a revision and expansion of a book that first appeared in 1985; *Pittsburgh's Bridges: Architecture and Engineering* (1999); and

*Henry Hornbostel: An Architect's Master Touch* (2002). A small volume in Arcadia's "Images of America" series on Oakland, written by Walter in partnership with the Pittsburgh History & Landmarks Foundation and the Carnegie Library of Pittsburgh, was published in 2005. His memoir, *Beyond the Surface: Architecture and Being Alive*, was published by the Foundation in 2006 and includes a select bibliography of his works.

Throughout his career Walter wrote articles and edited books and manuscripts. As the Pittsburgh History & Landmarks Foundation's architectural historian, he wrote frequently for *PHLF News*, prepared historic survey documents, represented the Foundation at City Historic Review Commission hearings, participated in architectural tours, and provided research and reference assistance to patrons of the Foundation's James D. Van Trump Library. His knowledge was encyclopedic, and his views on architecture were always exactly stated.

His legacy will live on through the Walter C. Kidney Library and Publications Fund of the Pittsburgh History & Landmarks Foundation, established through a bequest from Walter and augmented by memorial contributions from friends and admirers. The fund will support the James D. Van Trump Library (to which Walter donated some 4,000 volumes comprising his private library) and the creation of publications celebrating the architectural heritage of the Pittsburgh region.

# Epilogue

Our settlement in this ancient terrain, this wild and spacious place, is a mere incident in its duration. Yet while we are here, let us enjoy what we have brought into being, the scatterings of little white houses, the engineering works, the monuments to matters large and small, the beautifications of the land, the occasional quiet masterpieces of the building art.

It will take no third Ice Age to eliminate what we have built. A demolition, a cheap and heedless remodeling, or simple neglect will do this at any time.

Walter C. Kidney, 2005